AUDIO
ACCESS
INCLUDED

VIOLIN

PIRATES OF THE CARIBBEAN

T0081549

Speed • Pitch • Balance • Loop

To access audio visit:
www.halleonard.com/mylibrary
Enter Code
2103-9161-8438-0659

ISBN 978-1-4234-2202-0

WALT DISNEY MUSIC COMPANY

DISTRIBUTED BY

7777 W. BLUEMOUND RD. P.O. BOX 13819 MILWAUKEE, WI 53213

Visit Hal Leonard Online at
www.halleonard.com

THE BLACK PEARL

VIOLIN

Music by KLAUS BADELT

BLOOD RITUAL/
MOONLIGHT SERENADE

VIOLIN

Music by KLAUS BADELT

DAVY JONES PLAYS HIS ORGAN

VIOLIN

Music by HANS ZIMMER

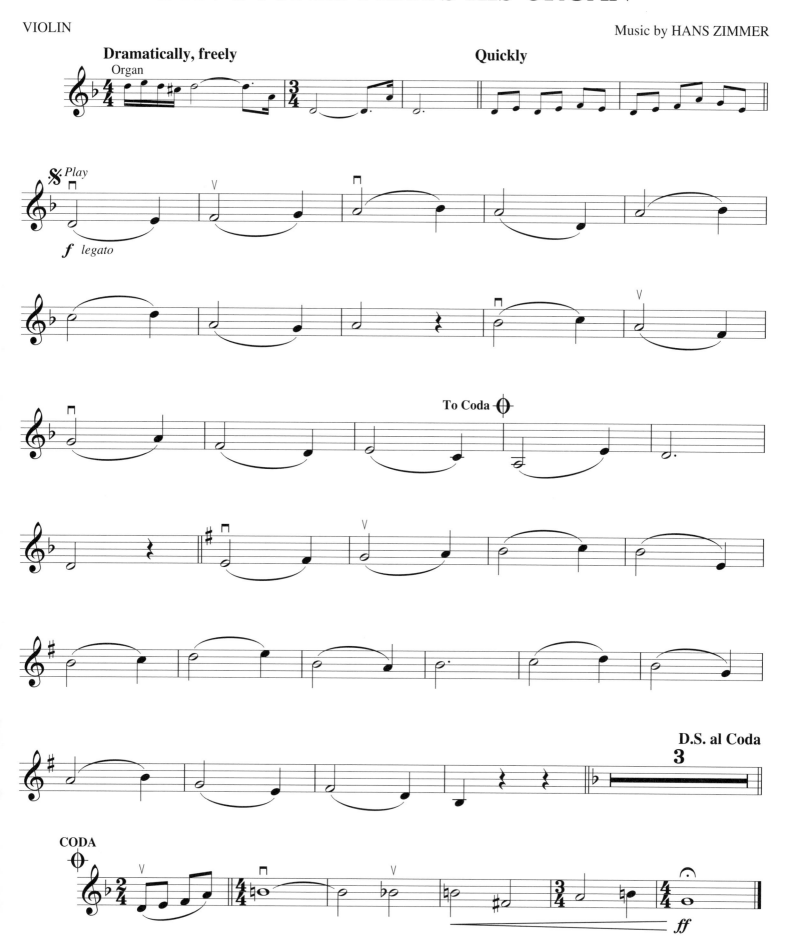

DAVY JONES

VIOLIN

Music by HANS ZIMMER

DINNER IS SERVED

VIOLIN

Music by HANS ZIMMER

I'VE GOT MY EYE ON YOU

VIOLIN

Music by HANS ZIMMER

HE'S A PIRATE

VIOLIN

Music by KLAUS BADELT

JACK SPARROW

VIOLIN

Music by HANS ZIMMER

THE KRAKEN

VIOLIN

Music by HANS ZIMMER

THE MEDALLION CALLS

VIOLIN

Music by KLAUS BADELT

ONE LAST SHOT

VIOLIN

Music by KLAUS BADELT

TO THE PIRATE'S CAVE!

VIOLIN

Music by KLAUS BADELT

TWO HORNPIPES
(Fisher's Hornpipe)

VIOLIN

By SKIP HENDERSON

WHEEL OF FORTUNE

VIOLIN

Music by HANS ZIMMER

UNDERWATER MARCH

VIOLIN

Music by KLAUS BADELT